My Work in Progress

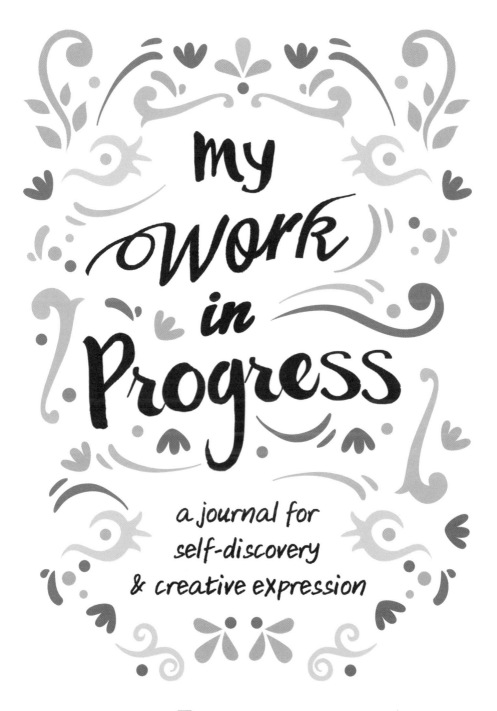

My Work in Progress

a journal for
self-discovery
& creative expression

ZONDERVAN®

ZONDERVAN

My Work in Progress
Copyright © 2020 by Zondervan

Requests for information should be addressed to:
Zondervan, *3900 Sparks Dr. SE, Grand Rapids, Michigan 49546*

ISBN 978-0-310-77067-1

Cover direction: Cindy Davis
Interior design: Denise Froehlich
Contributor: Estee Zandee

Printed in Malaysia

20 21 22 23 24 / IMG / 10 9 8 7 6 5 4 3 2 1

Introduction

Writing is one of the few things that cuts through the humdrum of our everyday, crazy-busy lives. While the world spins at a hectic pace and the list of things we have to do keeps growing, writing gives us the chance to pause, reflect, create, and discover—to savor and celebrate life.

Whether you're a master writer or if this is the very first book on writing you've picked up, this is your invitation to say hello to creativity and invite it into your daily life.

Much like creativity itself, this book doesn't have many rules. It doesn't matter where you start, or how you progress. Write, doodle, and scribble all over the pages as much or as little as you like. Feel free to tailor these prompts to your liking. All that's asked is that you approach each page with earnest fun—that delightful mix of taking each page seriously enough to do the activities but with a flare of curiosity and adventure.

Let's get started!

Flex Your Awesomeness

"JUST BE YOURSELF, THERE IS NO ONE BETTER."

—TAYLOR SWIFT

Most of us would admit that we have a few winning characteristics, but that's just scratching the surface! Your awesomeness goes deeper than you know. Fill up this page with positive statements about yourself. And don't overthink—just keep writing.

I am amazing.	I am _____
I am strong.	I am _____
I am smart.	I am _____
I am _____	I am _____
I am _____	I am _____
I am _____	I am _____
I am _____	I am _____
I am _____	I am _____

Just look at all that awesomeness! Dog-ear this page so you can always go back to it as a reminder of your amazing self.

Dream a Little Dream

Think back to a dream you had recently, or one that has stayed with you. Make a quick sketch if you like. Then write it out—all the strange, ridiculous details and the feelings they brought up. As you write, ask yourself:

⊕ Was the dream in color or black and white?

⊕ What was the weirdest part?

⊕ Where were you when you had the dream?

⊕ What do you think prompted the dream?

"dReaMS, if THeY'Re any GOOd, aRe alWays a LittLe Bit CRaZY."

—RAY CHARLES

SO ROOMY

The spaces we live in show evidence of who we are, what we value, and how we spend our time. But we're so used to seeing the same walls, windows, and furniture that we rarely think about them . . . until today. Select your favorite room in your home, find a comfy spot, and start writing about what you see. Think about the level of messiness and the decoration style. What does this room reflect about you and the other people who've entered it? What memories are stored here? What do you notice first and what's unexpected about this room?

Jarred

"Courage is knowing what not to fear."

—PLATO

What makes you the most afraid? We all have a few things that keep us up at night or plague our thoughts and decisions during the day. We may not ever be completely rid of our fears, but we can put a lid on them to keep them from plaguing our minds. Place your fears in the jar and enjoy your new sense of freedom.

Color Theory

"Mere color, unspoiled by meaning, and unallied with definite form, can speak to the soul in a thousand different ways."

—OSCAR WILDE

Throughout history, people have used colors to symbolize specific emotions. Even today, we use colors very strategically to communicate feelings. But not every shade means the same thing to everyone. For example, red symbolizes love and romance in some cultures, but to others it means war and violence. Talk about opposites! In each of the colored circles, write the emotion it stirs up in you. Then on the lines below each circle, write out why you feel that way.

Color in Action

Write a short story about anything you want, using as many colors on the previous page as you can to give emotional vibes and undertones to your story.

Plot Twist

We've all read a story or two that didn't end the way we felt it was supposed to—the couple that shouldn't have gotten back together, or that character who shouldn't have died. Well, this your chance to rewrite that ending. Pick a story you want to "fix," using the same characters and setting, then write the last scene the way you wish it had happened.

Cheers!

It's time for a toast! Write a few paragraphs in honor of your best friend or a family member. Put all your most eloquent words to use and praise the characteristics, talents, and strengths in them that you admire. Reminisce about funny or meaningful moments you shared together and thank them for being in your life. Extra cheers for ripping out the page and giving it to the person you wrote about.

Compliment Collection

"a COMPLIMENT IS VERBAL SUNSHINE."

—ROBERT ORBEN

Fill the sun with all the good things people have said about you. Even if you have a hard time believing some of these statements, write them down anyway. Now sit back and soak up all that golden sunshine!

ALL IN THE DETAILS

Select a favorite keepsake or an object that means something to you. Use lots of flowery words and colorful descriptions to write down everything about it—what it looks like, where it came from, what makes it special to you and why. Take your time and enjoy the process.

Aromatherapy

What is your hands down favorite smell in the whole world? Maybe it's the scent of a summer rainstorm, the aroma of your mom's famous recipe, or the unique fragrance of a good book. Whatever it is, think about that scent until you can practically smell it for real. Then translate that smell into words. Pull out all your descriptors here, and if a memory comes to mind, write about that too.

Switcheroo

> *"Beautify your inner dialogue."*
>
> —AMIT RAY

What are the messages you frequently tell yourself—the not-so-great phrases that play in your head on repeat? Use the chart below to switch out those phrases for life-giving, empowering words.

The next time you find yourself playing the same old phrases on repeat, switch that tired tune out with your new message.

Phrases I tell myself	What I **should** tell myself (because it's true)

GRATITUDE

"The more grateful I am, the more beauty I see."

—MARY DAVIS

Gratitude is like a secret power—it elevates our attitude, lifts our perspective so we can take in all the good things in our lives, and transforms normal, everyday things into miracles. Make a list of all the things you're grateful for. Nothing is too big or too small. If you need more space, fill up the margins with gratitude.

1. _____
2. _____
3. _____
4. _____
5. _____
6. _____
7. _____
8. _____
9. _____
10. _____
11. _____
12. _____
13. _____
14. _____
15. _____

16. _____
17. _____
18. _____
19. _____
20. _____
21. _____
22. _____
23. _____
24. _____
25. _____
26. _____
27. _____
28. _____
29. _____
30. _____

Wind Down

"To hear, one must be silent."

—URSULA K. LE GUIN

Settle into a comfortable but attentive sitting position, set a timer
for five minutes, and enjoy the silence. Don't hum a tune, try to
think, or plan your day. When a thought comes up, let it float
on by like a leaf in the breeze. When the timer sounds, write
about your experience. Was it difficult or easy? Did the time
pass fast or slowly? What emotions did you feel? Did your
mind keep circling back to certain thoughts?

Guilty Pleasures

We all have them. Maybe it's a weakness for sweet treats, binge-watching shows, or a need to check social media whenever your phone is close. Maybe it's getting and sending gossipy texts, downing energy drinks, or some other vice you use to get through the day. Fill in the orbs with the "felonious" habits you turn to. Circle the guilty pleasures that could make you a better person if you gave them up. And in the lines on the next page, write about why you think you have that particular vice in the first place and what you like about it. What would be hard about giving it up, and what would be good?

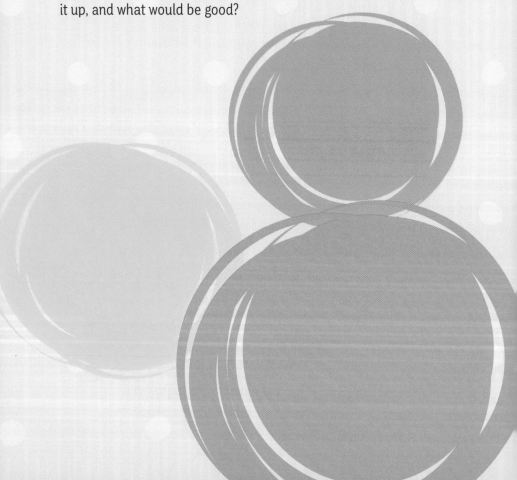

"NEVER TAKE LIFE SERIOUSLY. NOBODY GETS OUT ALIVE ANYWAY."

—SYDNEY J. HARRIS

Nothing jolts our sense of perspective quite like remembering our own mortality. We're all going to die eventually, but that doesn't mean we'll be forgotten. The influence our life has on others and the world around us will outlive us—and it's bigger than we think. Write out a list of things you want to be remembered for. Is there anything on this list that doesn't match your life right now? What small steps can you take today to align the two?

Throwback

"Sometimes you will never know the value of a moment until it becomes a memory."

—DR. SEUSS

Let's throw it back—way back. To your first-ever memory. Write down the earliest thing you can remember. How old were you? What was happening? Who were you with? Was it a sad memory or a happy one? How have you felt the subtle influence of that memory throughout your life?

ALPHABETICAL

Creativity often shows up in the most unexpected places—especially in situations with (seemingly) the most limitations. Try out this activity and see for yourself. Write a fun sentence about anything you want on each of the lines below, *but* the first word has to start with the corresponding letter of the alphabet. Each sentence can stand alone or connect with each other to tell a story. You might just be surprised at the words you come up with.

A _____

B _____

C _____

D _____

E _____

F _____

G _____

H _____

I _____

J _____

K _____

L _____

M _____

N _____

O _____

P _____

Q _____

R _____

S _____

T _____

U _____

V _____

W _____

X _____

Y _____

Z _____

Brand-New World

Book a ticket to a country of your own creation. Let your imagination run wild and fill this new land with anything and everything you want. Describe what this new country is like and make some notes in the categories below.

Who lives here and what do they do?

_____

_____

_____

What is the food like?

_____

_____

_____

What special holidays and traditions do they celebrate?

_____

_____

_____

What is the landscape and weather like?

_____

_____

_____

What is unique about this country?

_____

_____

_____

Rise and Shine

Reflect on how the last few mornings have gone for you and write down your normal routine in the first chart below. No judgment! In the other chart, write down how you would *like* your morning routine to go. Do a quick check to make sure your ideal plan is realistic for your life right now, then compare the differences and write down your observations.

Normal Morning Routine

Time I wake up	What I do to get ready/How things go

Ideal Morning Routine

The time I'd like to wake up	How I'd like to get ready/How I'd like things to go

Identify one small adjustment you can make to get a wee bit closer to starting your days off the way you want.

The adjustment I'd like to make

Gallery of Inspiration

Inspiration comes in many forms and people—some from those alive and close to us, some heralding from the halls of history, and still others coming to us from celebrity stages. Reflect on the individuals who have inspired you in some way and write their names in the frames. Dog-ear this page so that the next time you need some inspiration, you can easily find this gorgeous gallery.

Trail Markers

"DON'T GO THROUGH LIFE, GROW THROUGH LIFE."

—ERIC BUTTERWORTH

Culture likes to tell us that we need to check off specific trail markers to walk this journey of life successfully—markers like *finish high school*, *graduate college*, *get married*, *buy a house*, and many others. But those milestones don't always make sense for everyone, and they for sure don't guarantee success or happiness. The road of life looks different for each of us and we all walk it the best we can. Fill in the lines above with milestones from your own life. Give yourself a pat on the back for how far you've come and celebrate the uniqueness of your journey.

Sweet & Sour

"Life is like a box of chocolates. You never know what you're gonna get."

—FORREST GUMP

No one has to tell you that life isn't all rainbows and hugs. No matter what stage of life you're in, even if it's a pretty good one, it comes with its own blend of sweet and sour. Think about your day-to-day routine—be it work, school, or time spent with friends, family, or even a special someone, etcetera—and name the sour things that cause you to feel frustrated, disappointed, or annoyed on the candies. Now think through the same categories and write down the sweet things that make you feel grateful, accomplished, or happy on the chocolates. Take a second to savor the unique flavor of this time in your life.

Dear Body

"Love your body and teach your mind to respect it."

—ANONYMOUS

The most intimate and daily relationship you have is with your body. You share everything with it, from secrets to stress. Like any other relationship, the one with your body can be complicated. We have unmet expectations for our bodies, and sometimes our bodies cannot do what they were made to do. Write a letter to your body and try to express how you feel about it. Write down what you like about it and what you dislike. Be sure to end with gratefulness, because no matter how complicated this relationship is, you're able to write today because of all that your body does for you.

Dear Body,

_____

_____

_____

_____

_____

_____

Sincerely, Me

Tasteful Memories

"Pausing for a meal together is such an easy way to say I love you."

—CHEF EMERY CHAPMAN

Our growling bellies so often bring us to the table, where we share food with others and create memories. Whether it's Thanksgiving dinner with your entire family, a late-night fast food run with friends (where you laughed so hard, milkshake came out of your nose), a unique dish shared in a different country, or brunch by yourself, meals go beyond just what we eat. Think back to a meaningful meal and describe it below. What was the setting, what did you eat, and who were you with? What made that particular meal so special?

In the Name of Love

"A more loving world will open up to us once we realize that everyone loves a little differently."

—ANONYMOUS

The English language only has one word for love, but there are many ways of showing love to our friends, family, and significant others. Maybe you express love by planning elaborate adventures or by spending hours sitting beside your favorite human in front of a fun show. Or perhaps you show affection by giving lots of hugs or calling a family member to share a funny story. How do you show love the most?

_____

_____

_____

Now select someone close to you—a significant other, a sibling, or a best friend—and write down the ways they show you love.

_____

_____

_____

Secret Talent

"Talented people almost always know full well the excellence that is in them."

—CHARLOTTE BRONTË

Humans are insanely weirder, smarter, and more talented than we think. So this is your chance to show off and write about the ability or talent you have that no one knows about. Nothing is too small, too weird, or too niche!

_____

_____

_____

_____

_____

_____

_____

_____

_____

_____

_____

_____

_____

CHECKUP

Let's do a little self-checkup, shall we? Like going to the doctor regularly to make sure our bodies are healthy, this is a simple exercise to make sure we're healthy all around. Spend a few moments listening to your mind and emotions. Honestly color in the category bars based on how well you feel you're doing (more color = the better you feel). Remember, you can be honest here. No one else will see this unless you want them to.

Money

Health

Mental Health

Emotional Health

Fitness

Friends

Family

Work/School

What stands out as you look at the results of your personal checkup? What small action do you prescribe to yourself for the improvement of your health in one area?

"Be The Reason Someone Smiles Today."

—ROY T. BENNETT

Fill this page with the things that are guaranteed to make you smile.

Top Hits

"Where words leave off, music begins."

—HEINRICH HEINE

Songs carry us through tears and laughter. Great music motivates us and gets us dancing. Meaningful lyrics comfort us and help us put feelings into words. Whether new hits or old classics, lyrical or instrumental, write down your favorite songs to create your own personal top ten hits list.

1. _____
2. _____
3. _____
4. _____
5. _____
6. _____
7. _____
8. _____
9. _____
10. _____

Mentor/Mentee

"Leaders are more powerful role models when they learn than when they teach."

—ROSABETH MOSS KANTOR

Our social worlds are full of people who serve as examples for how to live life well. Coworkers, teachers and coaches, fellow students, brothers and sisters, aunts and uncles, and even our friends serve as role models of what to do or what not to do. We're always learning and growing from others—sometimes in formal mentor/mentee relationships, and other times in casual situations where we listen and watch others. Who are the people you are learning from? And who may be looking up to you?

Mentors

_____

_____

_____

Mentees

_____

_____

_____

Party Time!

"Let each day be a festival of joy."

—RAVI V MELWANI

Create a holiday to celebrate something special to you. Nothing is off-limits—it could be a national celebration of a historic event or the anniversary of a meaningful moment. Or maybe it's a party for your dear pet or a daylong recognition of your favorite dessert. Select something you want to celebrate and have fun imagining festive decorations, special foods, and party traditions.

Party Planning List

Autograph, Please!

"If I'm gonna tell a real story, I'm gonna start with my name."

—KENDRICK LAMAR

Your name is unique. Even if you spell it the exact same way as a hundred other people, your name means something special to your friends and family, and especially to you. Write the family history behind your name as well as its meaning (look it up if you don't already know). Ask yourself if you've always liked your name—why or why not? Then reflect on what your name means to you and how it shapes your life.

Your autograph:

What Your Name Means to YOU

Beyond the Comfort Zone

"You are braver than you believe, stronger than you seem, and smarter than you think."

—A. A. MILNE

There's a lot of hype about going outside of our comfort zone, that bubble we like to live in that feels familiar, secure, and safe. Staying inside the bubble seems like the best thing to do, but we have an inkling that better things await us just beyond its confines. The thing is, you've already have gone outside that comfort zone. In fact, the reason you know you have a comfort zone is because you've stepped outside of it from time to time. Name those times you moved out in bravery, faced the scary unknown, or accomplished the bold thing.

_____

_____

_____

_____

_____

_____

Free Write

"I write because I don't know what I think until I read what I say."

—FLANNERY O'CONNOR

Free writing is the amazingly simple technique of giving yourself permission to just write. Free writing helps us shake loose from the ways we hold back our thoughts or stifle our ideas. So write without stopping until you've filled the page. Put down whatever comes to mind. It doesn't have to make sense, and it doesn't have to all go together. Don't think, and definitely don't overthink. Enjoy the freedom!

FOR THE WORLD

"People who are crazy enough to think they can change the world are the ones who do."

—ROB SILTANEN

What is one issue in the world you want to see resolved? Perhaps you're passionate about a particular human right or the environment. Maybe you long to see a cure discovered for a disease or for all hunger to end. What need makes your heart beat a little stronger and causes you to search for answers? Why do you feel connected to this particular need? What is one thing you can do to make a small difference?

Dream Chasing

"The future belongs to those who believe in the beauty of their dreams."

—ELEANOR ROOSEVELT

Dreams are wonderful, inspiring things—motivating us to be better people and to do great things.

But not all dreams are worth chasing. Some are just pie in the sky—fun ideas but more distracting than achievable. Write down your dreams and then mark them with the shape that applies the best.

What's one thing holding you back from achieving your dreams?

DREAM—Pie in the sky(★) or Can't wait to do (♥)

Dear · · ·

There's something very special about getting a handwritten note. It takes time to put pen to paper, to craft a meaningful or fun message to make someone's day. Try it now. On the next page, write a letter to a friend or family member. Say hello, possibly throw in a funny story, and tell them how much they mean to you. End your letter with an invitation to be pen pals. Cut around the dotted line, pop it into an envelope, and post it knowing you brightened that person's day with a little connection.

TIP: Letters are a great way to reconnect with someone you haven't talked to in a while.

So Misunderstood

"By BeinG yourSelf, you Put SOMeThinG Beautiful into THe WORld THat waS not THeRe BeFoRe."

—EDWIN ELLIOT

Being misunderstood is a lonely, sometimes painful feeling. Yet we can get strangely used to it. What do others commonly misunderstand about you? Take note of the emotions that get stirred up in you. What do you think is behind the misunderstanding? How can you clear the air?

_____

_____

_____

_____

_____

_____

_____

_____

_____

Happy Place

*"The world is full of beautiful places.
Let your heart be one of them."*

—JENIM DIBIE

What is your ideal happy place? Maybe it's a real place you've visited, a favorite room, or your childhood home. It could be a place in your imagination—somewhere you go when you need a sense of security and safety. Recall this special place and describe what it looks like. What about it makes you feel happy and safe?

Look at You Grow

"Be patient with yourself. You are growing stronger every day. The weight of the world will become lighter . . . and you will begin to shine brighter. Don't give up."

—ROBERT TEW

We learn and grow a little every day. These micro changes add up to big differences. Think back five, ten years ago. How have you changed since then? In what ways have you stayed the same?

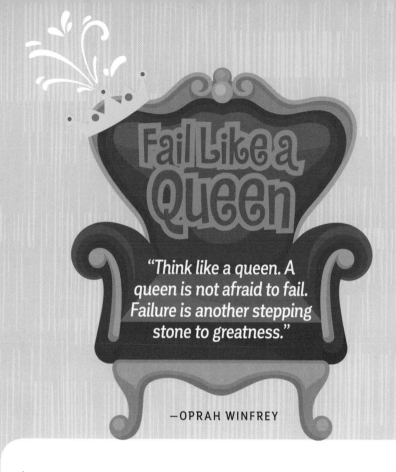

Fail Like a Queen

"Think like a queen. A queen is not afraid to fail. Failure is another stepping stone to greatness."

—OPRAH WINFREY

An epic wipeout, a massive screwup, a total catastrophe—we've all failed at some point or another. Write about a time when you got up close and personal with failure. Go into all the gory details. What was your big takeaway from that experience?

Guess what—you survived! You're here and you're stronger and smarter now. Write a little "good job" note congratulating yourself on your fail and on becoming the queen you are today.

Tell Me, Please

"I learned that telling the truth is a big part of loving yourself."

—IYANLA VANZANT

Have you ever wished someone would tell you that you're rockin' this life thing? Have you ever craved a friend's comforting words, or longed to hear someone apologize or say, "I forgive you"? There are probably a dozen things you deserve to hear. But here's something important: You don't have to wait for someone else to say them. You know what your heart needs to hear in order to thrive. Take the space below and give yourself permission to write, and receive, the words you need.

The Reframe Game

"Sometimes a change of
perspective is all it takes
to see the light."

—DAN BROWN

Sometimes it feels like being human just means having to do things you don't want to do. We have to complete chores, we have to keep our homes clean, we have to go to school, we have to go to work . . . We get so preoccupied with the have-to's that we miss the get-to's—the little ways we have the opportunity to contribute to the world through everyday tasks. In the first column, write down those pesky things you have to do that bore you to death or frustrate you to no end. Then, using the second column, reframe the have-to as a get-to—the hidden opportunity to make the world a little better.

HAVE-TO	GET-TO
I have to clean my living space.	I get to make a comfortable and clean space where I enjoy to be and can welcome others into as well.

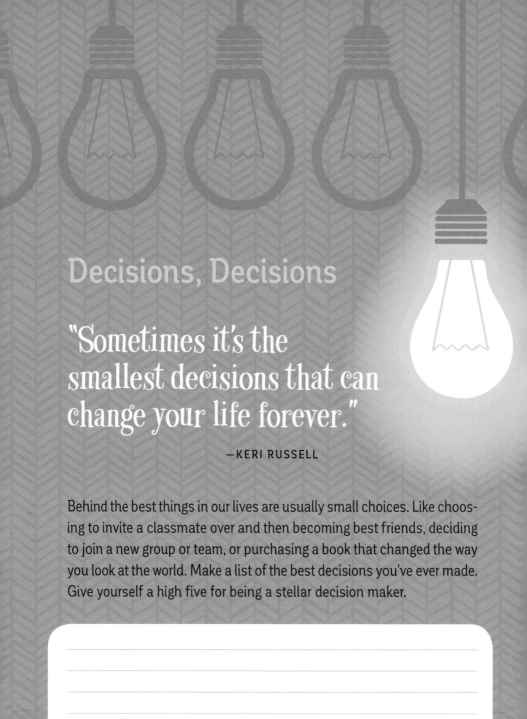

Decisions, Decisions

"Sometimes it's the smallest decisions that can change your life forever."

—KERI RUSSELL

Behind the best things in our lives are usually small choices. Like choosing to invite a classmate over and then becoming best friends, deciding to join a new group or team, or purchasing a book that changed the way you look at the world. Make a list of the best decisions you've ever made. Give yourself a high five for being a stellar decision maker.

CONSIDER THIS...

Our brains are always active, planning the next move, thinking through the task at hand, coming up with something good to say . . . But every now and then, the speed of activity slows and we have space to focus on other things. When your brain isn't busy, what do you think about? What thoughts, plans, or wonderings do you have hanging around in the background of your mind?

Character

"There's as many atoms in a single molecule of your DNA as there are stars in the typical galaxy. We are, each of us, a little universe."

—NEIL DEGRASSE TYSON

You read about them, you see them in movies, and now it's time to make one of your own. Use your imagination to create a character. They can be absolutely whatever you want them to be. Feel free to draw a portrait of your new friend, and let the prompts below guide your imagination process.

Character's name: _____

What is their personality like? _____
_____

What do they look like? _____
_____

Where do they live? _____
_____

What are they afraid of? _____
_____

What are their special talents? _____
_____

What do they want? _____
_____

Never, Ever

Make a list of the things you've never ever done but you want to do someday. And then make a list of things you will never ever do again, or ever do at all.

HAVE NEVER DONE

WILL NEVER DO

Book Lover

Since humans first invented paper and bound it together between two covers, books have changed people's lives. What book changed the way you see and interact with the world? What about that book was so moving to you? Write about it on the cover below.

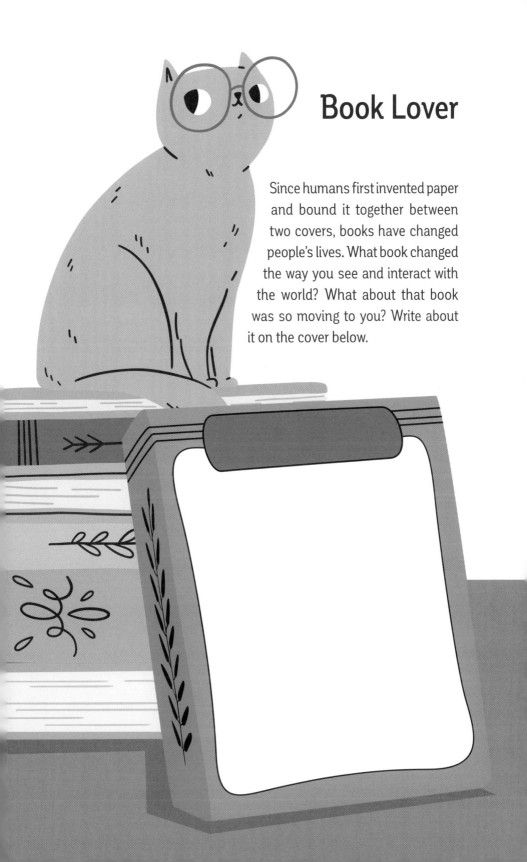

Up to the Challenge

"It's not the absence of fear. It's overcoming it."

—EMMA WATSON

Life comes at us with all sorts of challenges. Sometimes we have physical obstacles to overcome, while other times we face daunting tasks in school or work. Challenges rise in relationships and even in our own emotions and thoughts. But you've already overcome more challenges than you realize. Use the chart below to reflect on the way you've busted through old challenges, and then prepare for the future.

PREVIOUS CHALLENGE	HOW I OVERCAME IT

FUTURE CHALLENGE	HOW I WILL OVERCOME IT

First

Make a list of all your wonderful firsts—for example, the first movie you saw in a theater, the first time you tasted coffee and hated it (or experienced love at first taste), the first time you kissed, the first time you drove a car, or the first time you took a trip by yourself. Let the memories carry you back as you celebrate all the things you've tried and started.

The first time I _____ .

The first time I _____ .

The first time I _____ .

The first time I _____ .

The first time I _____ .

The first time I _____ .

The first time I _____ .

The first time I _____ .

The first time I _____ .

The first time I _____ .

The first time I _____ .

The first time I _____ .

STORYBOARD

"Good ideas are common—what's uncommon are people who'll work hard enough to bring them about."

—ASHLEIGH BRILLIANT

You know all those fun writing ideas floating around in your head—those stories, character plans, creative projects, and what if's and could be's? This is the place to write them all down. There's something life-giving, inspiration-sparking about giving your ideas a place to reside. So have fun with this project, and remember no idea is too small or too out of the box to be listed here.

Ask Away

"Many things are lost for want of asking."

—GEORGE HERBERT

We can go an awfully long time carrying an unasked request inside us. Maybe we need to ask for forgiveness or have to ask for clarity. Perhaps you need to ask for a raise, a second chance, or a change. The sense of putting ourselves out there to make the request or the fear of what the answer might be can hold us back. But with a little reflection, you'll likely find you have everything you need to ask away. Write about the request you need to make. What's holding you back? What will you do if the answer is yes? What will you do if the answer is no?

_____

_____

_____

_____

_____

Haiku to you

"You can find poetry in your everyday life, your memory, in what people say on the bus, in the news, or just what's in your heart."

—CAROL ANN DUFFY

Haikus are the best! They're such a fun way to express short thoughts in a creative way. Plus, since it's a form of poetry, you might feel pretty impressed with yourself when you write one. Traditionally, haikus are about nature, but this is your haiku we're talking about. Write whatever you like. Here's the only rule: haikus are made up of three lines—five syllables in the first, seven syllables in the second, and five again in the third.

I love the haiku
So elegant and honest
I will write one more

Now you try:

_____
(FIVE SYLLABLES)

_____
(SEVEN SYLLABLES)

_____
(FIVE SYLLABLES)

Haikus are kind of addicting, so feel free to try out a couple more here.

_____
(FIVE SYLLABLES)

_____
(SEVEN SYLLABLES)

_____
(FIVE SYLLABLES)

_____
(FIVE SYLLABLES)

_____
(SEVEN SYLLABLES)

_____
(FIVE SYLLABLES)

_____
(FIVE SYLLABLES)

_____
(SEVEN SYLLABLES)

_____
(FIVE SYLLABLES)

_____
(FIVE SYLLABLES)

_____
(SEVEN SYLLABLES)

_____
(FIVE SYLLABLES)

CAPTION THIS

Stories are quite literally all around us. Find an intriguing photograph in a magazine, on a book cover, or on social media. Let your mind ponder the image for a minute and imagine what could have happened to lead up to that particular picture, or what happened right after. Write down the story your imagination came up with, complete with dialogue and descriptions.

Share Kindness

"kindness is free. Sprinkle that Stuff everywhere."

—ANONYMOUS

No one has to tell a writer like you how powerful words can be. They can build someone up, share helpful knowledge, and comfort someone you might not even know. On the next page, write down an encouraging note. Pour all the kindness you can into it because we never know what sort of difficulty someone is going through. Rip the page out and put it in your pocket. Carry it around with you as you go about your day until you feel the moment is right, then leave your note as a kind surprise for someone else to find.

if you need encouragement ...

Work, Work, Work

"My mission in life is not merely to survive, but to thrive; and to do so with some passion, some compassion, some humor, and some style."

—MAYA ANGELOU

We spend a lot of time doing our work and attending school, but we very rarely get a chance to really stand back and think about it for a minute. Whether you're in the middle of a work project or school exams, write how you generally feel about what you're doing now. What's your favorite part? What is most challenging about it? How do you think you're doing? What changes would you like to see?

Beautiful Things

The saying is true: beauty is in the eye of the beholder. So what catches your eye? What things in life do you find truly beautiful? Make a list here and dog-ear the page so that whenever you feel a little jaded, as though there's nothing good and beautiful in life anymore, you can turn here and remember there are positives after all.

Liar, Liar

The lies we hear—from ourselves and from other people—are heavy things. If we start to believe them, they weigh down our thoughts and dreams. Write the lies you've been told on the rocks and then write what's *actually* true around the beautiful succulents. Get rid of those nasty lies by coloring in the rocks. Now enjoy the view of your colorful garden.

Surprise!

"Surprise yourself every day with your own courage."

—DENHOLM ELLIOTT

Life has a way of throwing surprises at us—some happy and some not so happy. Write about something unexpected that happened to you. What occurred, or didn't? How did you feel in the moment—and how do you feel now? What did this experience show you about yourself, about living, and about others?

Peeved, I'm sure

We all have those little annoyances, those pet peeves that get under our skin. From open-mouth gum chewing to someone kicking the back of your chair to being interrupted—we bump into these pests all the time. Name your pet peeves, then give them a nod. Yes, they're weird and they're petty, but they're yours.

Banner of Truth

"But I suppose the most revolutionary act one can engage in is . . . to tell the truth."

—HOWARD ZINN

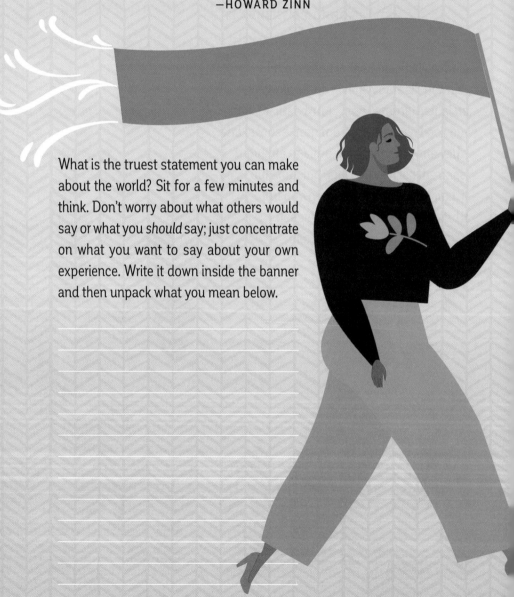

What is the truest statement you can make about the world? Sit for a few minutes and think. Don't worry about what others would say or what you *should* say; just concentrate on what you want to say about your own experience. Write it down inside the banner and then unpack what you mean below.

HEAR ALL ABOUT IT

Write an ad for your favorite product, book, or show. Make sure to explain what this particular thing does, how it does it, and how it makes your life easier, better, or more fun. Pull out all those shiny marketing words. (Check out some ads in magazines or on social media if you need some ideas to get started.)

Coffee Date

"ONE GOOD CONVERSATION CAN SHIFT THE DIRECTION OF CHANGE FOREVER."

—LINDA LAMBERT

Imagine you're at a classy café, sipping your favorite beverage. Across the table from you sits a historical person you've always wanted to chat with. Write out the conversation you would have together.

POWERFUL

"There's nothing quite as powerful as people feeling they can have impact and make a difference. When you've got that going for you, I think it's a very powerful way to implement change."

—ANNE M. MULCAHY

We may not think of ourselves as powerful as we go about our lives, but we have more power and sway than we think. And we often can find evidence of it when we look back at all that we've accomplished, when we stand up for ourselves, when we protect others, or when we want to give up but keep trying anyway. Make a list of the things that make you feel like the powerful person you are.

Adapt This!

"Creativity involves breaking out of established patterns in order to look at things in a different way."

—EDWARD DE BONO

Adaptions and retellings are a fun way to let our imaginations loose and get our creativity going. Write a folk story or a fairy tale. Then circle all the nouns—the people names, places, animals, and objects. Swap them out with brand-new ones and read your story again. Which version is more intriguing? Continue to swap out the nouns until you have a story you really enjoy.

Mystery Solved

> *"Life is infinitely stranger than anything which the mind of man could invent."*
>
> —ARTHUR CONAN DOYLE

What happened to Amelia Earhart? Where is the lost ark of the covenant? What is the true story behind King Arthur or the lost city of Atlantis? Use your imagination to solve one of these unanswered tales or to tackle another famous mystery. Write out your thoughts or put them into story form.

_____
_____
_____
_____
_____
_____
_____
_____
_____
_____
_____
_____
_____
_____
_____
_____
_____

Chitchat

"In true dialogue, both sides are willing to change."

—THICH NHAT HANH

Create a dialogue between three characters. Follow the conversation where it leads you, but avoid using the word *said*. Instead, use gestures and actions to show which character is speaking and words that show *how* the characters are talking, such as shouted, whispered, begged, whined, demanded, cried, and muttered.

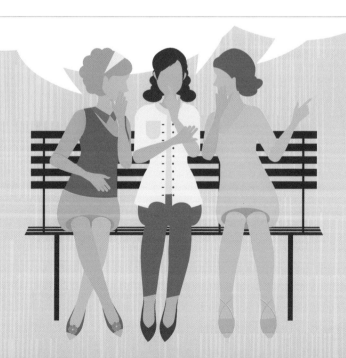

Head vs. Heart

"A good head and a good heart are always a formidable combination."

—NELSON MANDELA

It is that natural connection between the head and the heart that enables us all to process life, make decisions, and live fully. But we all lean on one part more than the other. Do you tend to think or feel your way through life? What is good and helpful about your mode of processing? What is challenging, and what do you feel you might miss out on from the other side?

GOOd OL' daYS

"Nostalgia is the heart's way of reminding you of something you once loved."

—RANATA SUZUKI

Nostalgia catches us all from time to time, calling up unique feelings and memories. Through the taste of a family recipe, the crunch of fall leaves, the smell of a campfire, or the melody of an old song, we are reminded of the past and long for those simpler, better days. What comes to mind when you think of the "good ol' days"? What do you miss? What do you long for the most?

Rhyme Time

"Why the world is just eager
For things that you ought to create
Its store of true wealth is still meager
Its needs are incessant and great."

—BERTON BRALEY

Create a list of four pairs of rhyming words (eight words total), like *park* and *lark*, *create* and *relate*. Now connect them all together to create a poem, ordering the rhymes so that they will match up with their pair on every other line. The goal is to have fun channeling your inner poet, however, so feel free to swap out rhymes and reorder pairs as you go, or create a different rhyme scheme all together!

1a. _____ 2a. _____ 3a. _____ 4a. _____
1b. _____ 2b. _____ 3b. _____ 4b. _____

_____ (1a)
_____ (2a)
_____ (1b)
_____ (2b)

_____ (3a)
_____ (4a)
_____ (3b)
_____ (4b)

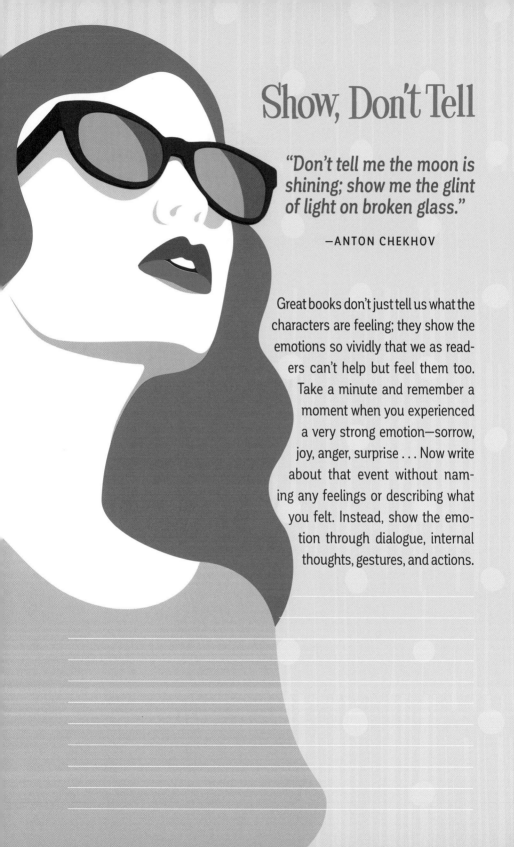

Show, Don't Tell

"Don't tell me the moon is shining; show me the glint of light on broken glass."

—ANTON CHEKHOV

Great books don't just tell us what the characters are feeling; they show the emotions so vividly that we as readers can't help but feel them too. Take a minute and remember a moment when you experienced a very strong emotion—sorrow, joy, anger, surprise . . . Now write about that event without naming any feelings or describing what you felt. Instead, show the emotion through dialogue, internal thoughts, gestures, and actions.

A Point of Defense

"You never really understand someone until you consider things from his point of view."

—HARPER LEE

Curiosity is one of the most powerful aspects of writing because it helps us understand others. Briefly write down an idea, concept, or belief that you strongly disagree with. Then switch sides and write a defense for how someone could argue that idea might actually be true and perfectly reasonable.

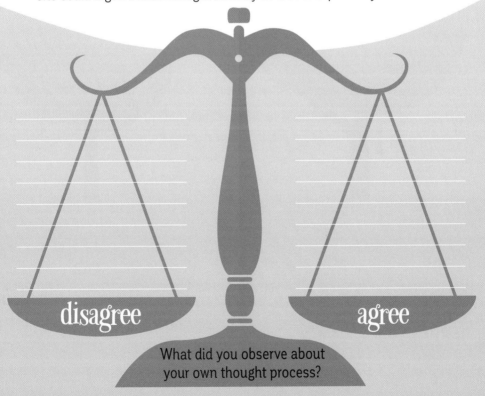

disagree

agree

What did you observe about your own thought process?

Time Travel

Pick a public place you visit often, a place you're pretty familiar with—such as a favorite coffee shop, the library, a public bus stop, or the local convenience store. Write a few sentences describing what it looks like today. Now step back in time and imagine what it would have looked like fifty years ago, a hundred years ago. What would have been there two hundred years ago?

Modern day

Fifty years ago

"Society grows great when old men PLANT TREES whose SHADE they know they shall NEVER sit in."

—GREEK PROVERB

One hundred years ago

Two hundred years ago

All in Good Time

"The best thing about the future is that it comes one day at a time."

—ABRAHAM LINCOLN

Night owls, early birds, afternoon pigeons ... Our bodies and minds are designed to reach optimal peak at unique times of the day. Knowing when we're at our best helps us organize our schedules according to our strengths. Reflect on how well you feel and how focused you are during the day. What part of the day is your favorite? When are you at your finest, your most productive, your most alive?

_____

_____

How can you adjust your daily routine to work better with your peak time?

_____

_____

_____

_____

seasonal Goals

"Live in each season as it passes; breathe the air, drink the drink, taste the fruit, and resign yourself to the influence of the earth."

—HENRY DAVID THOREAU

Summer, fall, winter, and spring—each season offers its own selection of fun activities. Whatever time of year you're in, make a short goal list of the things you want to do and see before the season changes.

1. _____

2. _____

3. _____

4. _____

5. _____

6. _____

PERSONIFY

"It's beauty that captures your attention; personality that captures your heart."

—OSCAR WILDE

We learn early on to give personality traits to well-loved objects. We played pretend with our toys and held conversations with our stuffed animals. And now we continue that habit by giving human personalities to things around us—such as talking to our cars, laptops, and potted plants. Pick an object you see every day, like your cell phone, mug, or trinket. Write what its human persona would look like. What kind of personality would it have? How would it talk and what would it say to you?

Word Count

"My aim is to put down on paper what I see and what I feel in the best and simplest way."

—ERNEST HEMINGWAY

Writers frequently face the task of writing about important or complex things with a very limited amount of words. They're constantly searching for more efficient, more accurate words to communicate precisely what they mean. The common rule is *less is more*. Think about a significant moment in your life. Now take a cue from Hemingway and write it out in as few words as possible while still capturing the experience. When you're done, read it over and scratch out any words that don't need to be there. Replace weak words with stronger, more precise words.

More Than Sight

Whenever we sit down to describe places and people, our first instinct is to write down what we see. But we humans have more than one sense; our understanding of the world is shaped by what we hear, smell, taste, and feel—the dog barking across the street, the perfume of flowers, the flavor of gum, and the warmth of the sun. Take this book on a walk around your neighborhood and jot down everything you hear, smell, taste, and feel.

Hear _____

_____

Smell _____

_____

Taste _____

_____

Feel _____

_____

Hello, Earth

"Being weird is a wonderful thing."

—ED SHEERAN

Imagine an alien just landed on Earth. They've never seen our technology, watched our social practices, listened to our music, or tasted our food before. They wouldn't know the "right" names for anything. To them, everything is strange and a little weird. Write about this curious alien's first day.

_____
_____
_____
_____
_____
_____
_____
_____
_____
_____
_____

Just the Essentials

The belongings we keep close at hand tell a lot about who we are as people. From the computer we use every day to the pair of shoes that expresses who we are, things shape the way we live. Make a list of your essentials—those things you use every day that you can't go without, which help you live your best life. Is there anything on that list that doesn't truly belong? Is there anything missing that *should* be there?

Life Rules

"I follow three rules: Do the right thing, do the best you can, and always show people you care."

—LOU HOLTZ

Rules keep countries, groups, and the world running smoothly. We create rules for ourselves too, sometimes without noticing it. Maybe you're the person who always arrives fashionably late, or the one who leaves early. Maybe you always make sure to color coordinate your outfit or make a point to wear a statement piece. Maybe you call your friend each week and always tell the truth. Write down your personal rule book below.

Knock, Knock

"I tried to catch some fog, but I mist."

—UNKNOWN

It's time for some comedy. Writing jokes can seem intimidating, but with a little practice, we can always find our way to the punch line. To get started, write answers to the following prompts:

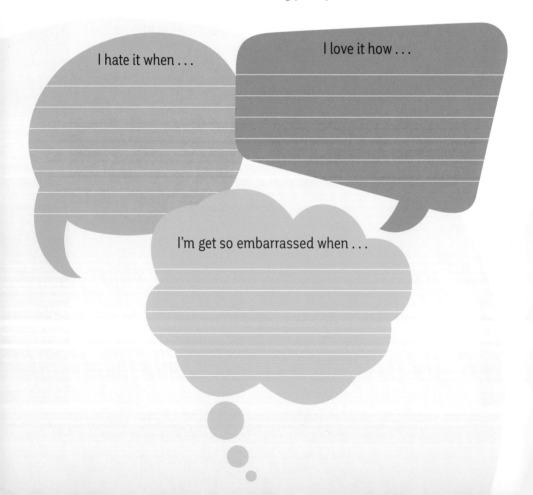

I hate it when . . .

I love it how . . .

I'm get so embarrassed when . . .

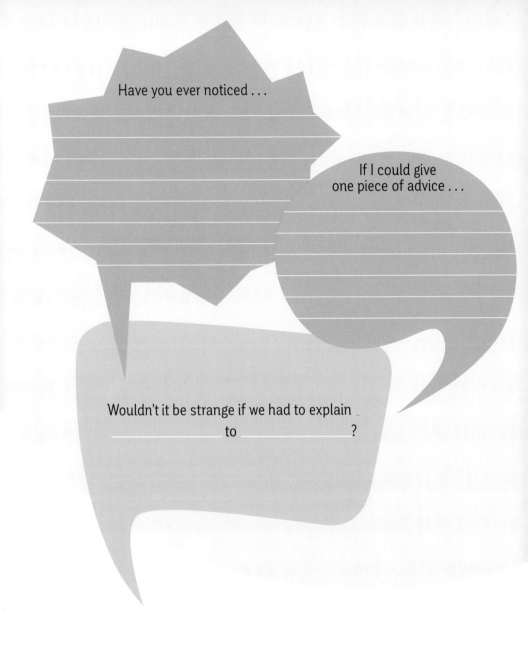

Now play around with your answers. Swap them with each other, reverse the sentences, add or remove a word. Try answering them again with sarcasm. Continue switching things up until you find something that sparks humor.

Worry Clouds

"Why worry? If you've done the very best you can, worrying won't make it any better."

—WALT DISNEY

Worries have a way of following us around and blocking out our sun like sad little clouds. The only way to dissipate them is to acknowledge why they are there. Write down all the things you're worried about.

Now that you can see what's got your skies so gray, ask yourself, what's filling your worry clouds with rain? What's fueling your worry? Is it desire for control, desire to be liked, or some other unmet need? Is it concern and love for those around you? Write it down. Tell your worries, "Thanks for trying to help, but I've got it from here."

_____

_____

_____

_____

_____

_____

_____

_____

_____

_____

Lift Me Up

"I'm beginning to recognize that real happiness isn't something large and looming on the horizon ahead, but something small, numerous, and already here. The smile of someone you love. A decent breakfast. The warm sunset. Your little everyday joys all lined up in a row."

—BEAU TAPLIN

A compliment, some progress on a big project, a delicious meal, a meaningful conversation—little joys like this do so much to shift our focus from what's going wrong in our lives to what's going right. Label the balloons with things that have lifted you up lately.

Looking at your balloon bundle of joy, what patterns do you see? Did you feel lifted up after spending moments with people, or during moments in quiet spaces? While creating, or while resting? How can you incorporate more of these things into your week?

Question Quest

"Good questions inform, great questions transform."

—KEN COLEMAN

Make a list of the questions you would like answers to. They can range across the board from a question about your past or your future to something broad about the world and your place in it to something niche, like the history of buttons. Tap into your curiosity and let it wander and wonder.

tune in to inspiration

"Music gives a soul to the universe, wings to the mind, flight to the imagination, and life to everything."

—PLATO

Turn on a playlist or the radio. When a song catches your interest, pay attention to the lyrics and the emotions conveyed through the music. Write out the scene that comes to mind as if you stepped inside the song. Let your imagination fill in any gaps.

"Creative people do not see things for what they are; they see them for what they can be."

—JULIE ISRAEL

Write down six terrible jobs. They might be the dirtiest or the most boring, or just the least interesting to you. Now imagine what could make them the greatest job after all. For example: an accounting clerk . . . but for dragons!

Job 1: _____

_____

_____

_____

Job 2: _____

_____

_____

_____

Job 3: _____

_____

_____

_____

Job 4: _____

_____

_____

_____

Job 5: _____

_____

_____

_____

Job 6: _____

_____

_____

_____

Nature + soul

"When you do things from your soul, you
feel a river moving in you, a joy."

—RUMI

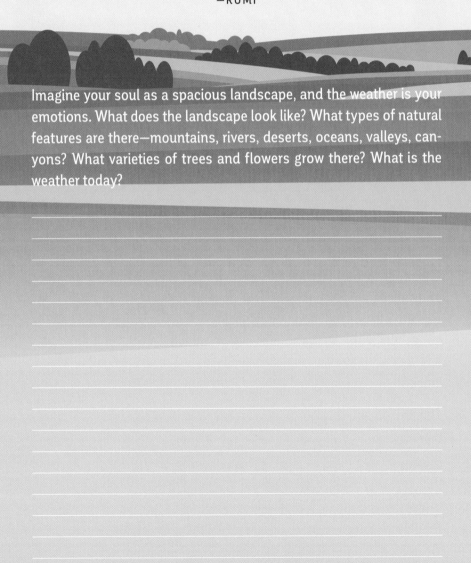

Imagine your soul as a spacious landscape, and the weather is your
emotions. What does the landscape look like? What types of natural
features are there—mountains, rivers, deserts, oceans, valleys, can-
yons? What varieties of trees and flowers grow there? What is the
weather today?

"**MUSIC** *is the way our memories sing to us across* time."

—LANCE MORROW

The songs we hear on the radio, share with friends, sing to in the shower, and dance to at celebrations make up the soundtrack of our lives. They capture a bit of the mood of special moments in our stories. List the songs that made up the soundtrack of your life.

Track 1: _____

Track 2: _____

Track 3: _____

Track 4: _____

Track 5: _____

Track 6: _____

Track 7: _____

Track 8: _____

A NEW ANGLE

Think about yesterday, or any recent day of your choosing, and write about it from someone else's point of view. Think about how the day would have looked and felt like from the perspective of your pet, a plant, a neighbor, or an entirely different person.

_____

_____

_____

_____

_____

_____

_____

_____

Fresh Start

> "It is never too late to be what you might have been."
>
> —GEORGE ELIOT

It's never too late for a fresh start. Every day gives you a new chance to begin again. If you could start over, what would you do differently?

_____

_____

_____

_____

_____

_____

_____

_____

_____

_____

_____

_____

_____

_____

Master in the Making

Whether it's learning a new language, gardening, or calligraphy, make a list of all the things you want to learn and master one day.

1. _____
2. _____
3. _____
4. _____
5. _____
6. _____
7. _____

Circle one you want to work on now, and note one small step you make toward mastering it today.

Language Skills

Don't worry, this isn't about grammar . . . at least not using the English language as you know it. Today, you get to form your very own language! To start, place a new symbol or marker underneath each letter below to create a new alphabet of your own design.

A B C D E F G H I J K L M N O P Q R S T U V W X Y Z

You might find it fun to create a unique, slightly different set of markers for vowels.

Now think about creating common punctuation marks and communication helps, like how English uses capital letters to show when a new sentence starts and places a period (or other mark) when the sentence ends. Add any of your favorites to the top of the chart.

. , ! ? " " ( ) – ; :

Things to think about:

Try it out! Write a paragraph or two about anything you want and see how your new language works.

Give your new language a name: _____

Character Fusion

Much of creativity comes from a curiosity to play with elements you already have—like when creating a fusion character. A fusion character combines the traits of existing characters to create a completely new one. Fill out the brief character profiles below using characters you like. For a truly interesting fusion character, choose a variety of base characters, like an animated one, a fictional one, and a person from real life—such as a neighbor or friend.

Character 1

Name:

Physical Description:

Skills and Strengths:

Weaknesses:

Character 2

Name:

Physical Description:

Skills and Strengths:

Weaknesses:

Character 3

Name:

Physical Description:

Skills and Strengths:

Weaknesses:

Now circle the character elements above that you find the most interesting. Fuse them together into a new character. Play around with different combinations and use your imagination to fill in any gaps.

"Creativity is the fun of putting together unexpected ideas."

—HAZEL EDWARDS

Fusion Character

Name: _____

Physical Description: _____

Skills and Strengths: _____

Weaknesses: _____

"Relationships grow like plants. They need to be watered."

—IDRIS BELO-OSAGIE

cultivate

Just like flowers, every relationship grows, blossoms, and goes through seasons of change. Write down the positive relationships you have with your friends, siblings, parents, teachers, neighbors, and anyone else you're connected with. Draw a little flower next to the ones that have grown strong and healthy. Circle the relationships that need some watering.

What's one small way you can sprinkle a little water on the relationship that needs it most?

NEWSWORTHY

"It ain't whatcha write, it's the way atcha write it."

—JACK KEROUAC

Put on your journalist cap and write about a fun event you attended, an exciting game you watched, or a new announcement you learned about. The first rule of journalism is to make sure to include the five Ws and H: Who, What, Where, When, Why, and How.

Creativity Spark

"Your potential is endless. Go do what you were created to do."

—UNKNOWN

Take a minute and reflect on your relationship with creativity. How does your creative spirit show up in your life? In what ways has it grown or changed in the last few years, or even the last few months? What are a few simple ways you can cultivate creativity into your life?

Now, write
about
anything
you want!